Walks Along the Ridgeway

ELIZABETH CULL

SPURBOOKS LIMITED

Published by:
SPURBOOKS LIMITED
1 Station Road
Bourne End
Buckinghamshire

© SPURBOOKS LTD. 1975

Maps reproduced by permission of the Ordnance Survey:
Crown copyright

I S B N 0 902875 52 3

Printed by Maund & Irvine Ltd., Tring, Herts.

Contents

Introduction

THE Ridgeway Long Distance Footpath was officially opened at Coombe Hill, near Wendover on 27th September, 1973. It runs for 85 miles from Overton Hill in Wiltshire to Ivinghoe Beacon in Buckinghamshire, crossing the Thames at Goring Gap, and is marked along the way by sturdy oak signposts, low stone plinths and white-painted "acorn" waymarks. The trackways it follows were old before the Romans came, having been in continuous use since man first travelled across the face of Britain. Indeed, the Ridgeway is thought to be the oldest prehistoric track in the country. The Path, and these walks, then, take the rambler to some historic and prehistoric landmarks.

Separated by the Thames, the two halves of the Path are very different in character. From a walker's viewpoint the Chiltern end is far more attractive, traversing as it does some of the prettiest walking country in England. The best walks lie between Ivinghoe and Watlington, and Goring has the river, which is beautiful in all seasons. Once into Berkshire the underlying chalk asserts itself; the Ridgeway is open to riders and cyclists as well as walkers, the going is harder underfoot and can be slippery in wet weather. But the view across the Vale from the high downs is inspiring; the Path runs straight as an arrow from Streatley to Overton Hill, and one can see the largest Chambered Barrow, the oldest carved chalk figure, and the most spectacular prehistoric temple in Britain along the way.

These Ridgeway walks are covered by the Ordnance Survey 1:50,000 maps Nos. 173, 174, 175 and 165. The maps in this book are reproduced by permission of the Ordnance Survey.

To walk the length of the Ridgeway from Overton Hill to Ivinghoe will be the winter pipe-dream of many and the spring-time realisation of the lucky few; this book tells you how to enjoy over 20 walks along the Ridgeway, even if the only time you have to spare is a few hours on a Sunday afternoon. You will see some lovely countryside, stride high hills, tramp through leaves on clean-floored beechwoods, come unexpectedly upon marvellous views, and where your feet pass will have passed the feet of your forebears, generation upon generation.

My own favourites are the walks around Watlington, Wainhill and Whiteleaf, but all are enjoyable, all will give you pleasure. I have given, in the bibliography, a list of books about the Ridgeway and the Chilterns, which will, I believe, add greatly to your enjoyment of this beautiful part of England.

ELIZABETH CULL, 1975

Area 1

Avebury, Silbury Hill, West Kennett,
Overton Hill, Avebury—3, 5, 4 or 7 miles

AREA 1

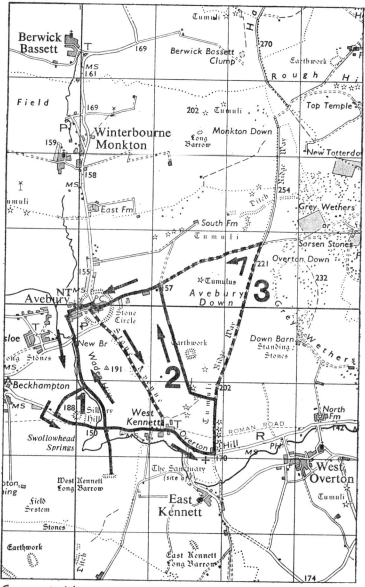

Scale 1:50,000

Area 1

Avebury, Silbury Hill, West Kennett, Overton Hill, Avebury
3 miles, 5 miles, 4 miles or 7 miles

How to get there: Bristol Omnibus Service No. 471 from Swindon or Devizes, or No. 476 Calne-Marlborough.
By car, A361 Swindon-Devizes road, or A4 Marlborough-Cippenham, turning on-to B4003 at East Kennett.

Refreshments: The Red Lion, Avebury, or the excellent snack bar in the Church Hall run by the ladies of the parish on Sundays and Bank Holidays.

What to see: The church, museum and Stone Circle in Avebury; Silbury Hill; the Sanctuary; West Kennett Long Barrow; the start of the Ridgeway Long Distance Footpath.

THE Ridgeway Footpath starts at Overton Hill on the A4, 5 miles west of Marlborough. Surprisingly, there is nothing to mark the start except one of the familiar stone Ridgeway plinths and a Ridgeway signpost, just as at Ivinghoe there is nothing to mark the end. However, within a two mile radius of Overton Hill lie the great Stone Circle at Avebury, the strange, conical mound of Silbury Hill, and the West Kennett Long Barrow. Thousands of visitors come every year to view these antiquities, and it is a comparatively simple matter to combine this viewing with a walk along the Ridgeway Path.

3 mile walk
Starting from the Red Lion crossroads in Avebury, walk through the village, and past the church to a house opposite, set slightly back from the road with three steps up to the front door. Turn left along the narrow path beside it, and go

on through the kissing gate at the end and across the field to another gate at the far side, giving onto the road. Here turn right along the road for 20 yards to where a signpost opposite irects you across a farmyard to a gate in the right hand corner, and on up the footpath ahead. Silbury Hill is clear before you, and less than half a mile brings you to a gate on the right and a bridge over the River Kennett. Cross the bridge and follow the broad, grassy path across fields, through two more gates, and onto the A4 by a garage. Silbury Hill is now on your left, 100 yards along the road. The plaque erected by the Ministry of Works tells us that the Hill is 130ft. high and its base covers five and a half acres. It consists of chalk rubble dug from the huge ditch which once surrounded it, and which was once as deep as the hill is high.

The walk continues along the main road for 200-300 yards, over the River Kennett again, until, just this side of a thatched cottage, a kissing gate takes you right onto a signposted footpath to the West Kennett Long Barrow, the largest chambered tomb in England. Only part of the tomb is excavated, but you won't be able to see much inside without a torch.

Rejoining the main road again, the 3 mile walk returns you to Avebury by the footpath 10 yards along the road on your right, opposite. The gate giving access to the path looks immovable, but in fact it opens quite easily. Over a stile at the end of the path, and on through a field beside the Kennett, with Silbury Hill now on your left, and carry on along the path back to Avebury, the way you came. *(End of 3 mile walk.)*

5 mile walk
To return to Avebury via the Ridgeway Footpath, turn right seeing the Long Barrow and walk along the road verge for the best part of a mile to Overton Hill, where the Long Distance Footpath starts. You will first pass the B4003 coming in on the left from Avebury, then the Ridgeway Cafe, also on the left. On the right there is the Sanctuary, once connected with the Stone Circle by the avenue of standing stones with which the B4003 keeps company, but now no more than a ring of markers in a field. It is opposite the

Sanctuary that the Ridgeway Path starts. Our route takes us for half a mile along the Ridgeway, where it turns onto the path coming in from the left. After another mile, where five paths join, you take the extreme left path which will return you to the Stone Circle and Avebury. *(End of 5 mile walk.)*

4 mile walk

If you have seen Silbury Hill and the Long Barrow and are intent only upon a walk along the Ridgeway, walk up the B4003 (Marlborough road) from Avebury following the standing stones of the Stone Avenue to the A4, where you turn left for the start of the Long Distance Footpath at Overton Hill. A 2 mile walk along the Ridgeway towards Hackpen Hill will bring you to a bridle-path striking away to your left, which if followed will bring you directly back to the Stone Circle. *(End of 4 mile walk.)*

7 mile walk

By extending the 5 mile walk along the Ridgeway, as in the 4 mile walk, you can enjoy a round walk of 7 miles.

Area 2

Uffington Castle, The White Horse,
Waylands Smithy—3 or 3½ miles

AREA 2

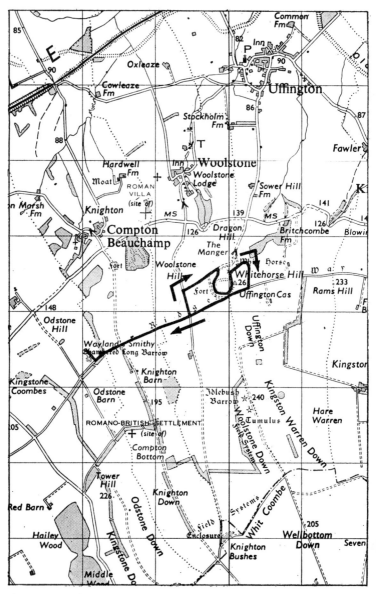

Crown copyright

Scale 1:50,000

Area 2

Uffington Castle, The White Horse, Waylands Smithy
3 or 3½ miles

How to get there: By car, B4507 from Swindon or Wantage, turning off at Uffington then following the road signs for White Horse Hill. No public transport is available.

Refreshments: Fox & Hounds at Uffington.

What to see: The White Horse of White Horse Vale; Waylands Smithy; the site of Uffington Castle.

TRACING the route of the Ridgeway Path on Ordnance Survey maps, one finds the words *Fort, Castle, Tumulus, Moat, Roman Temple,* scattering the ground invitingly. Unfortunately, even if one can pinpoint the site of the fort, castle or tumulus referred to, it frequently appears as little more than a few humps or hollows of no apparent significance. One looks hopefully, and goes home feeling cheated.

Not so at Uffington, where the ramparts of the Iron Age Castle are plain to see, though not so plain as the ancient White Horse carved into the chalk nearby. The best place from which to see the White Horse of White Horse Vale is Badbury Hill, itself an Iron Age site, 5 miles away to the north-east near Faringdon. However, Patrick Crampton, writing in 1962, tells us in his book "The Prehistoric Ridgeway" that from no point now can the Horse be seen in its entirety because the carving has sunk over the years and is now on different planes.

3 mile walk

This short walk starts from the car park, Map Reference 289865, at the top of White Horse Hill. Ignoring the direct, signposted route to the White Horse, make your way to the far end of the car park where a chalky path strikes uphill, left, through an iron gate, and turns right, up onto the ramparts of Uffington Castle. These mounds, enclosing a vast grassy hollow, are all that is left of the Iron Age fort, and as you walk the ramparts you can see the Ridgeway Path clearly, just below on your right.

Carry on round until you pass the Ordnance Survey Triangulation stone on your right, when you will soon find a path leading over the mound to the White Horse. This curious figure, looking like anything but a horse, is known to be over two thousand years old, and one wonders at the compulsion which has urged men to keep the 374ft. clear of grass and weed throughout this long, long time.

To resume the walk, climb back up the hill behind you, keeping the wire fence on your left, back past the Ordnance Survey point, to an iron gate ahead which gives onto the Ridgeway. Turn right for a walk of a mile or so along the Path to Waylands Smithy.

Here you are walking on the very summit of the downs, with all the valley spread out below you, and the Ridgeway Path stretching ahead, chalf-white across the hills. Waylands Smithy lies to the right of the path, and is clearly signposted, but long before you come to it you will see through the gaps in the hedge on your right the ring of beech trees that encircles the monument.

The legend of Waylands Smithy can be read in the paperback "Guide to Prehistoric Monuments in England and Wales", or in "Companion into Berkshire" by R. P. Beckinsale, and "History, People and Places in New Oxfordshire" by Frank Martin. Briefly, it is that any passing rider whose horse casts a shoe should tether the animal at the Smithy, leave a silver coin on the capstone, whistle three times and go away for ten minutes. Upon returning he will find the coin gone and his horse shod. Horse or no horse, this long barrow is worth seeing; the mound and many of the standing stones remain, though only the smaller of the burial chambers can be entered.

3½ mile walk

You can now either return along the Ridgeway to White Horse Hill the way you came, or vary the route by walking back along the Ridgeway to the point where the second pathway crosses—a paved path where you turn left. Three hundred yards along this road on your right, another road runs back between rippling cornfields to the White Horse car park.

The downs up here are marvellous for a picnic. The castle ramparts give shelter from the wind, the view across the peaceful Vale is inspiring, and everyone would have fun with a kite.

Area 3

Wantage, Letcombe Regis, Letcombe
Bassett, Wantage—3, $4\frac{1}{2}$ or $6\frac{1}{2}$ miles

AREA 3

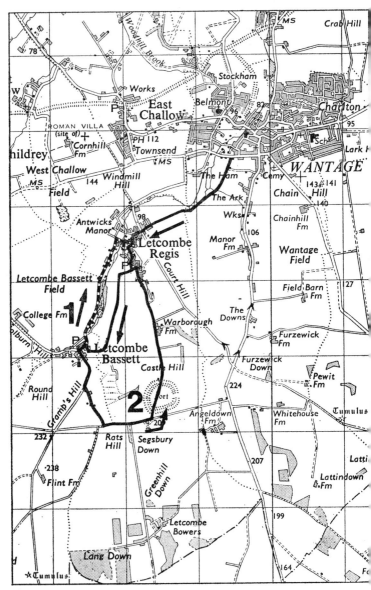

Crown copyright

Scale 1:50,000

Area 3

Wantage, Letcombe Regis, Letcombe Bassett, Wantage
3 miles, 4½ miles or 6½ miles

How to get there:	Thames Valley Bus Service from Reading to Wantage, or by car, A417 from Streatley, B4507 from Swindon.
Refreshments:	The Greyhound or the Sparrow in Letcombe Regis, The Yew Tree in Letcombe Bassett, King Alfred's Kitchen, Wantage, by the car park exit.
What to see:	Typical English villages of Letcombe Regis and Letcombe Bassett, thatched cottages, village inns.

THE ancient town of Wantage is famous as the birthplace of King Alfred, and to prove it, his statue stands in the market square. It is also one of the few places from which the Ridgeway can easily be reached without a car, as Thames Valley buses go there from Reading. For those travelling by car, there is a large, well-signposted car park off Portway. From Wantage we can walk up to the Ridgeway via the typically English villages of Letcombe Regis and Letcombe Bassett, with their wealth of thatch and timber.

For all walks

Our walk starts opposite King Alfred's Grammar School, where Portway becomes Ickleton Road. Here there is a narrow, paved path running off to the left, first between railings, then past a house on the left and across allotments, to Letcombe Regis. Keep to the paved path, ignoring turnings off, for about a mile. As you go, you will see the Letcombe Brook on your right. More will be seen of this brook later.

The path ends at a small block of houses, where you continue to the crossroads and then take the road opposite, signposted Letcombe Bassett. This road winds through the village of Letcombe Regis, past the Greyhound and several thatched cottages, to the church. Here you turn left at a sign, "Village and Downs only", for 200 yards or so, until you see a sign on the right "To the Ridgeway 1¼m." Follow this broad path for a short distance until you reach two footpaths on the left within 10 yards of each other. Take the second of these, a narrow path between hedges, which will bring you along in due course to the tiny village of Letcombe Bassett. At the first bend in the path, look down to your right and you will see again the Letcombe Brook, forming a pond and water-cress beds at this point. The path ambles along, looking down on the road below, sometimes with rabbits bounding before you, and in one spot with a particularly pretty view of a partly thatched white house, with the brook running past.

Eventually you come past a house on the left and down onto the road, where you turn left for Letcombe Bassett village. If you are taking the long walk you will turn left again by the Post Office where a sign says "Downs, No Through Road", but a little further on in the village is the Yew Tree Inn, ideal for refreshments, should you wish to visit it first.

For the short walk, turn right opposite the Post Office onto the Letcombe Regis road, which you follow for three quarters of a mile. Do pause for a while as you come to the watercress beds; the air is full of country sounds, moorhens walk on the water, pigeons flap and coo, there are dozens of different wild flowers to see, and everywhere is peaceful. Then a gentle ramble on to Letcombe Regis, not too much uphill, past pretty country cottages at one of which is kept geese and guinea fowl.

After three quarters of a mile you come to a group of farm buildings on your left, and on your right a footpath sign directing you past dainty, cream-painted cottages, over the bridge across Letcombe Brook, over a stile and across the field ahead. Walk to the top of this field, keeping the fence close on your left, and over another stile, when you will find yourself back on the broad track that brought you up from

Letcombe Regis village. Turn left and follow it through the village again, and back to Wantage the way you came.

4½ mile walk—can be extended

Those who take the longer walk will also find themselves finishing on this broad track, but not for some time. Having turned left by Letcombe Bassett Post Office, you continue uphill along the metalled road for roughly three quarters of a mile until it finishes on the Downs where the Ridgeway Path crosses. This route doesn't take us far along the Ridgeway itself, but it is a simple matter to extend the walk along the long-distance footpath in either direction, provided you mark your way down. The width of the Ridgeway, which is far wider than the usual footpath, is explained by the fact that it was for centuries a drove road, along which sheep and cattle were taken to market.

The route back to Letcombe Regis is left along the Ridgeway for quarter of a mile and then left again onto a footpath over a stile onto a swell of sheep-nibbled turf, and over the hill fort at Castle Hill. The signpost points you downhill over this turf towards a combination of two stiles and a gate. This negotiated, you carry on down the steeper hill in front of you, keeping the hedge to your right. Here one is really isolated, enclosed by the hedge on one side and the swell of the ground on the other. Yet another stile leads you to a really sharp rise and descent—keep a sharp look-out for rabbit holes. At the top of the rise, a stile on your right leads on to a very narrow path through a section of a wood for 100 yards or so, and over yet another stile into a meadow. Follow the hedge and fence around the meadow to your right for some 200 yards, until the footpath sign directs you through the split-rail fence on your right. One feels there should be a stile here, but the fence bars are wide enough to get through or stout enough to climb. This gives on to a footpath running left, which after a while becomes a broad, grassy path between cornfields, leading straight back to Letcombe Regis and thence to Wantage.

To shorten the walks

Either of these walks can be shortened by two and a half miles by driving from Wantage to Letcombe Regis.

Area 4

Blewbury and the Downs—6 miles

AREA 4

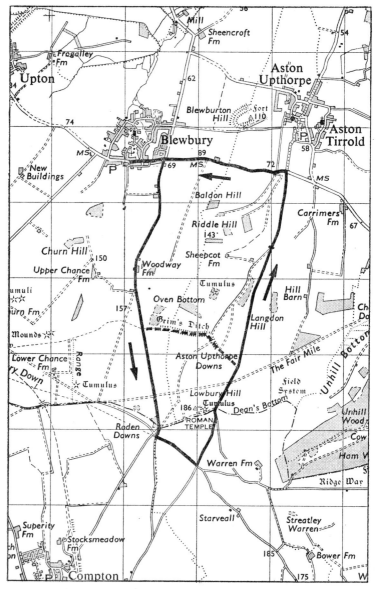

Crown copyright

Scale 1:50,000

Area 4

Blewbury and the Downs
6 miles

How to get there: By road, A417 Streatley-Wantage. By Chiltern Queen buses from Reading to Streatley, or Alder Valley buses from Oxford to Streatley, or Train service, Reading to Didcot line. Then Thames Valley bus service from Streatley.

Refreshments: The Blueberry Inn and the Barley Mow in Blewbury.

ONCE across the Thames the character of the Ridgeway changes. It is still the broad, chalky path we knew, but the leafy green Chilterns have given way to rolling golden downland, where the Path is isolated above the towns and villages in the valley below. There are many places along the B4507 running from Wantage to Wanborough where the Ridgeway is no more than two or three miles from the road. The sign "To the Downs" which we see at Bishopstone and Hinton Parva, and at Wroughton and Winterbourne Bassett on the A361, indicates this. Unfortunately a lack of supporting footpaths in most of these areas makes them rather unsuitable for the "round walks" treatment, though it is easy enough to drive up the access paths for a quiet stroll on the downs and along a stretch of the Ridgeway.

Here we have suggested a rather long walk, but you can shorten it at will. Blewbury, on the A417 Streatley to Wantage road, is used as the starting point for this walk because it is accessible by public transport. Thames Valley bus services from Streatley serve the area, and Streatley is just across the bridge from Goring, itself served by Chiltern Queen buses from Reading and by the Oxford-Alder Valley bus service, or by train (Reading-Didcot line).

From Blewbury, one walks along the High Street in the direction of Streatley as far as the Blewbury Service Station, then up the narrow, unsignposted road opposite Woodway Farm. The roadway finishes at the farm, and then the way leads straight on through the farmyard onto a broad, chalky track leading to the Downs. This leads past a section of Grims Ditch, on your right, and across the Fair Mile.

This path joins the Ridgeway after about 1¼ miles, at a point where five paths meet. The Ridgeway is the second on the left of these five paths, or the first on the right. Followed for half a mile to the left it leads to a particularly fine, open stretch of downland around the Aston Upthorpe estate.

The obvious path down from this stretch, should you wish to take it, will lead you back down to the road to Blewbury. This is almost three miles, and takes you past the sites of a Roman Temple, tumulus, and Grims Ditch, on your left. To avoid walking down the main road at the end, you can cut off left down the footpath through Grims Ditch and back via Woodway Farm.

Turn left at the bottom, and a walk of 1½ miles along the road will return you to your bus stop and give you a walk of 6–6½ miles in all. Unfortunately, there is no pavement and the verges are unreliable, so it is not recommended that you walk along this road with children. Much better to return to the Woodway Farm path by which you came up.

Area 5

Goring, South Stoke, Little Stoke,
Cleeve, Goring—$2\frac{1}{2}$, 6, 7 or $9\frac{1}{2}$ miles

AREA 5

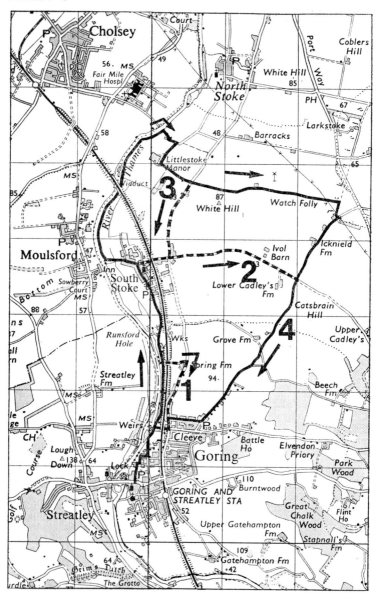

Crown copyright

Scale 1:50,000

Area 5

Goring, South Stoke, Little Stoke, Cleeve, Goring
2½ miles, 6 miles, 7 miles or 9½ miles

How to get there: By train—Reading to Didcot line. By bus—Chiltern Queen buses from Reading, or the Oxford-Alder Valley service to Streatley.

Refreshments: Numerous inns passed along the way; The Miller of Mansfield or the John Barleycorn at Goring.

What to see: The 11th century church at Goring; Cleeve Mill; the endlessly fascinating river.

This walk starts pleasantly along the river by Cleeve Mill, leaves it for a while to pass through the village of South Stoke, returns to the river banks along the water-meadows, leaving it finally by Little Stoke House to return to Goring along the Icknield Way. In its entirety it is a long walk, but instructions are given for shortening it at two points. This is not a walk for "the heat o' the sun or the furious winter's rages", but for early mornings before the sun is well up and the river paths are dewy and damp, or for later afternoons and evenings when the pubs are open. You will find it very different from the wooded ways and leafy paths at Wainhill, Whiteleaf and Watlington, but the river makes up for all, and dropping down into Goring in the twilight along the Icknield Way where you have probably not seen another soul in two miles is quite an experience.

2½ mile walk

Goring can be reached by bus or train, or there is ample room in the clearly marked car park behind Goring shopping centre. The walk starts at Thames Way, which is a few yards along on the right, past the Miller of Mansfield, just before the road crosses the river to Streatley. The Ridgeway Path runs along Thames Way after passing over the river, on its way to Wallingford and Watlington. Proceed along this pleasant road, where the Thames can be seen "running softly" beyond the houses on your left, until a white acorn mark on the fence post directs you into a narrow footpath at the end. Now one catches only tantalising glimpses of the river through gaps in the left-hand hedge or fence, but there is no continuous lower path. After a while your path emerges on to the road before Cleeve Mill, where the fascination of the racing mill-whel will slow your steps. Take note of the entry to the path you have just left; you will want to return through it later.

Continue along the road past Cleeve Mill for a short distance until it bears right, where you leave it and take the gravel path directly ahead, beneath the sign carved high on a pillar announcing that it is a "Private Carriage Road". You are still on the Ridgeway, which shortly develops into a leafy lane with a good view of the river and all about you the song of birds, and coots calling. After about a mile you come to "Ye Olde Leatherne Bottel", a famous Thames-side hostelry. You can shorten the walk here by turning right, over the Railway bridge, and straight on until you reach the B4009 crossing. Here turn right again and proceed along the verge for half a mile until the signpost for Cleeve Mill points you to the right. Take the path back past the Mill to Goring, giving you a walk of some $2\frac{1}{2}$ miles. *(End of $2\frac{1}{2}$ mile walk.)*

6 mile walk

Continuing the walk past "Ye Olde Leatherne Bottel", you take the signposted bridle way on to South Stoke, passing the Goring Thames Sailing Club on your left. Eventually this path takes you away from the river and across the fields into South Stoke. Carry straight on through the village, past the Free Church, the Garage, "The Perch & Pike" inn, the primary school and the Parish Church, where you have another opportunity to shorten the walk if you wish by turning right past the Parish Church to the B4009. Here you can either turn right again and return to Goring as described earlier. However, the road is a busy one and the verges cannot be relied upon. It is therefore recommended that you cross over and go up the lane opposite which will lead you, after about a mile, to the Icknield Way where it crosses just past Cadley's Farm. Turn right on to the Way, technically a motor road here, but with very few cars using it. After two miles you come into the village of Cleeve and where the B4009 crosses you will see the signpost to Cleeve Mill mentioned earlier, which you follow to return to Goring after a walk of six miles. *(End of 6 mile walk.)*

7 and 9½ mile walks

To continue the walk to Little Stoke adds to the route, giving walks of 7 or 9½ miles, but for a mile and a half you will be walking in the water-meadows along the edge of the river, so it is well worthwhile. You carry straight on past the church at South Stoke until a signpost on your left directs you round past Corner House and up a "No Through Road", to turn left again where the path forks, towards the river. Here the footpath turns right into the water-meadows and runs along the water's edge all the way to Little Stoke, so you can watch the boats passing up and down the river and see the water birds which previously you could only hear. The footpath ends at an iron fence where you turn right, passing the dovecotes, and carry straight on until you come to another path crossing. Turn right here, past Little Stoke House, and follow the road as it bears left and winds a little uphill to the B4009.

Here you have two choices; you can turn right on to the B4009 for half a mile until the signpost directs you to South Stoke village, where you turn left back to the Parish Church at South Stoke and return along the river path the way you came, giving you a walk of some seven miles in all. This is a very pleasant walk, much recommended. Alternatively, you can cross over the B4009 and take the bridle path opposite marked "Portway 1½m." This path rises gently uphill, with woods on your right and a cornfield on your left. The chalky bank of the cornfield is smothered with wild flowers of many varieties and pocketed with rabbit holes and other small animal homes. As the path drops down over the hill you see a farm in the valley below and a motor road ahead. The bridle path gives way to a footpath along the edge of another field, coming out eventually on to the road at an iron gate. Turn right here on to the Icknield Way, and return to Goring as previously described.

Area 6

Watlington Hill and Christmas Common—$3\frac{1}{2}$, $5\frac{1}{2}$ or 7 miles

AREA 6

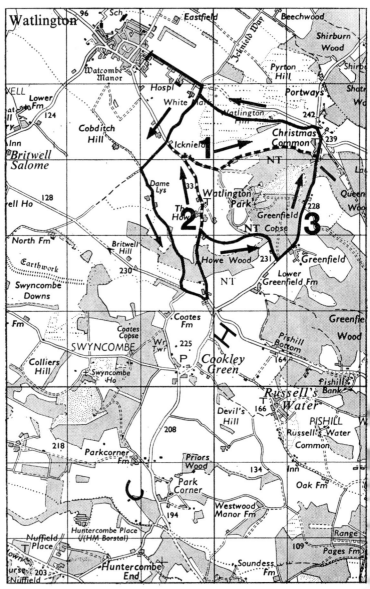

Crown copyright

Scale 1:50,000

Area 6

Watlington Hill and Christmas Common
3½, 5½ or 7 miles

How to get there: By road, M40 or Oxford Road to Lewknor and thence to Watlington.

Refreshments: The Jolly Ploughman, or Fox & Hounds along the route; The Black Horse in Watlington serves morning coffee; The Hare & Hounds by the Town Hall serves excellent lunches; and The Wishing Well Restaurant in Couching Street serves morning coffee and afternoon tea.

What to see: Watlington Town Hall and the 17th century houses in the High Street.

THREE miles from the M40 Lewknor turn off is Watlington, a pleasant, unremarkable Oxfordshire market town, with 17th century houses along the High Street and the cross-roads half obliterated by a superb open-arched Town Hall. Built in 1665 this Hall has original mullioned windows and a sundial clock on the south-west face.

The Ridgeway passes Watlington to the south-east, by the rise of Watlington Hill, and not far away is the intriguingly named village of Christmas Common. This group of walks starts from Watlington's good free car park (left at the cross-roads as you come from Lewknor). There is limited parking around the Ridgeway at the foot of Watlington Hill, and if you are able to park there it will cut one mile off any of the three walks. Distances are given from Watlington car park.

Leaving the car park, turn right on to the road, and passing "The Carriers Arms" with its dovecotes on the left, follow the road for half a mile, past the hospital, until you see the swell of Watlington Hill before you and Ridgeway Path signs pointing to left and right. This section of the route is described correctly, as the Icknield Way, in Ordnance Survey maps. Turn right on to the Ridgeway, and continue along the broad, grassy path until a minor road crosses. Those on the shortest walk will turn left here on to the road for not more than 200 yards to where a footpath sign on the left leads down past a bungalow with an enviable sunny front porch. Between this bungalow and the neighbouring house a narrow footpath dives into the trees, to take you around the south side of Watlington Hill. This path runs between hedges, over open turf and then between high banks, for about a mile, until it emerges on to the road to Christmas Common. In places, this part of the walk is quite superb. The turf is scattered with wild flowers, the view across the peaceful vale is worth walking miles to see, and when at last this view is left behind and the route is enclosed between high banks, these banks are fascinatingly pitted and tunnelled with a multitude of animal homes. Rabbits can frequently be seen, and I have even seen a weasel lolloping along to vanish down one of the holes, around the edge of which were the grisly remains of many meals.

When at last the Christmas Common road is reached, the walk takes us left. But you can, if you wish, turn right here instead and walk the few hundred yards round the bend in the road to the "Fox & Hounds" in the village of Christmas Common for refreshments, before finishing the walk.

Having emerged on to the road from Watlington Hill, you will see opposite a Royal Observer Corps observation post. Turn left here and continue along the road until you come to a short pathway on the left leading to a stile. Go over this stile and back on to the other side of Watlington Hill. Follow the obvious way across the Hill, bearing neither to right nor left, and within half an hour you will be back in the car park at Watlington. The obelisk cut into the chalk which you pass on the way down is thought to be 18th or 19th century, but of no known historical significance.

Leaving the Hill by a stile, you come down on to the road along which you walked from Watlington and which will lead you back, past the Ridgeway signs, to the car park.

5½ mile walk

For those on either of the longer walks, the route crosses the road where the short walk turns left and continues along the Ridgeway past the signpost saying "Dame Alice Farm". The path is now hard-surfaced, and in springtime the banks which enclose it are a mass of bright white stitchwort and yellow celandine. After half a mile we pass the gate of Dame Alice Farm—marked on the Ordnance Survey map as "Dame Lys". Now the way is soft underfoot and leafy, winding gently uphill. Stamp your feet here, and the damp earth responds with a hollow thud, firing the imagination with tales of subterranean passages and hollows hiding badgers, moles and rabbits, and reminding us that Kenneth Grahame wrote "Wind in the Willows" not so far away at Pangbourne.

Soon you are edging round farm fields, and leaving them behind you find yourself walking again through woods, along a bridle path. You have now left the Ridgeway; continue along the bridle path until the wood again gives way to fields, where you bear left for some 200 yards until a road crosses. A short distance left along this road you come to a T-junction; turn left again, and just opposite is the "Jolly Ploughman", waiting to refresh you along your way.

From here the route leads on past the "Jolly Ploughman" down the hill, a busy road, but after the first 100 yards or so you can walk in the edge of the wood.

Those on the 5½ mile walk should continue along this road for a mile or so until signposts show the Ridgeway crossing to right and left, turn right on to the Ridgeway, and return to Watlington the way you came.

7 mile walk

Those on the longest walk should continue down the hill past the "Jolly Ploughman" for about a quarter of a mile until, just by a "Road Narrows" sign, two paths are found leading into the wood on the right. Take the lower of these paths, which even in early summer is floored with rustly beech leaves, and where in spring the misty haze of bluebells can be seen, while if you look for them, violets can still be found hiding along the banks.

Bear left when the path forks, and you will be on firmer ground. In the spring, bluebells will be around you on all sides as far as the eye can see, their scent filling the air. Keep to the left again as the path forks, and continue until, after a dip and a rise, a house comes into view on the right. Bear round with the path past this house and continue ahead to the road. Your route now lies along this peaceful country road for the best part of a mile, through the village of Christmas Common, before rejoining the short walk to return home around Watlington Hill.

A little way along this road, opposite Greenfield Farm, a footpath sign invites you through a gate and back into the wood. Each time I go this way I am lured into the wood, convinced that I can find a way through to Watlington Hill. Alas, I never do, and always return defeated to the road by the Lodge Gates to Watlington Park where the estate path is bordered by vast patches of wood sorrel. If you have the time and energy, these woods are worth investigating. They are denser than the Buckinghamshire woods encountered on other walks in this book, with fewer birds, and seem quite vast in their silence.

However, although worth exploring, they do not form part of this walk, which leads on through the village of Christmas Common, turns left where the signpost points to "Watlington 1½m.", and left again at the next fork. Three hundred yards further along the road is the Royal Observer Corps post, where you rejoin the short walk to return to Watlington.

Area 7

Bledlow, Hempton Wainhill, Chinnor
Hill, Wainhill, Icknield Way, Bledlow
—$2\frac{1}{2}$, 5 or $6\frac{1}{2}$ miles

AREA 7

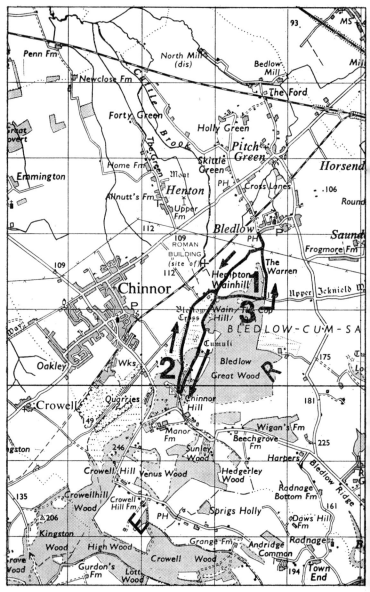

Crown copyright

Scale 1:50,000

Area 7

Bledlow, Hempton Wainhill, Chinnor Hill, Wainhill, Icknield Way, Bledlow
2½, 5 or 6½ miles

How to get there: From Chinnor, take the B4009 road to Princes Risborough. Two miles or so along the road turn right at Skittle Green cross-roads for Bledlow. "The Lions" is about half a mile down this lane. As an alternative, you can take the road signposted "Wainhill Only", some half a mile before the Skittle Green cross-roads. This leads you to the village of Wainhill, and peters out into a bridle path, and you would join the walk at the house called "Serenity". Driving along this road you get a clear view of Bledlow Cross cut into the woods above, but this is not suggested as a starting place because parking at the bridle path is very limited, and can cause a nuisance to the residents.

Refreshments: "The Lions" at Bledlow.

What to see: Bledlow Cross; Bledlow Church of the Holy Trinity. This is a Norman church with nave arcades dated c.1200, the remains of a medieval wall painting, and a carved Norman font.

THIS is a walk that can be anything you want it to be—a quiet evening stroll before opening time, a pleasant afternoon saunter, or an all day picnic with the children, exploring Wainhill, with lovely views to enjoy and pleasant walks before and after.

It starts from the oddly named "Lions of Bledlow", a pleasant country pub with ample parking space around it. I saw a peacock here on a misty November morning, and on the same walk, disturbed a partridge in the woods behind, which rose with a whirr and a clatter and a shriek, startling the wits out of me.

For all walks

With your back to the pub and the "Lions" sign in front of you, take the signposted footpath across the fields on your left (not the bridle path running down the side of the pub). This path runs between fields for a quarter of a mile or so, until it is joined by a bridle path coming in from the left. From here it continues as a gravel path between a sparse hedge on the right and a post and wire fence on the left. Continue along the gravel path, taking note of a black and white timber house away above the swell of the fields on your left, nestling in the shadow of the woods. You will pass the front of this house later, along the Icknield Way.

When you have walked about a mile in all you will be surprised to find the path apparently finishing at the front gate to a private house. Do not think you have lost your way and turn back, nor try to creep round behind the garage. Simply open the gate and walk through into the garden of the much publicised private house as the Ridgeway Path passes across its surrounding land. After you have passed through the gate you will see a cluster of signposts on your right, among which are the familiar carved "Ridgeway" signs.

2½ mile walk

If you are taking the short walk, having nothing more in mind than a pleasant, easy stroll back to the pub, you turn left after passing through the gate, walk across the front of the house and on to the broad bridle path now in front of you. Here there is a sign put up by the Buckinghamshire County Council which assures you that you are on the Icknield Way. This unmistakeable path leads you through a fine stand of beeches, past the front of the black and white house you saw from below, and round in a long curve back to Bledlow. Follow it until it is joined by a similar path bending in from the right. Here turn left, and you will come easily back between hedges of hawthorne and roses to the "Lions", where you started, having walked a comfortable 2½ miles or so.

5 mile walk

If you are taking a longer walk, turn sharply at the gate to the group of signposts on your right. Your walk will bring you back to this point later. For the moment, you are to take the most right-hand of the bridle paths down towards the village of Wainhill. The path runs, narrow but straight, for about 500 yards with houses occasionally visible through the trees, until it comes to a house lying close to the path on your right. This house is called "Serenity", and one can well see why. A few yards further on you come to another bridle path at a junction, where you turn left to climb up around the edge of Bledlow Great Wood to Chinnor Hill. Up in this wood on your left, some 200 yards or so past this junction, Bledlow Cross is carved into the chalk. The cross is plainly visible from Wainhill village below, but is not apparent from where you stand on the path. If you prospect around a bit in the woods up on your left you will probably find it, and if you have children with you, you may think it worth the search. Legend has it that if you run up and down and across it in bare feet it will give you energy to complete your walk. What it does give you are dirty feet!

The path through the woods is easy to follow, running as it does in a hollow with the woods climbing steeply on the left, and protected by a high bank on the right. Do pause occasionally to look back at the splendid view, but do not bother to climb the high bank to see the view that instinct tells you must lie to your right; you will have this spreading before you all the way back, and it is worth waiting for.

After a mile or so you come to a house on the right called "Windy Ridge". You will shortly be doubling back and looking out over the wood through which you have just walked, to the views beyond.

Now the path spreads out into a little green. High on the

trunk of a young oak on your left there is a sign saying "Nature Reserve". Bear sharp left at the oak tree, across a few yards of the green, and into the wood again at the path in front of you. There are in fact two paths here, one unmarked and one signposted "Bridle Path", and further on across the green there is an entry to the nature reserve protected by a fixed-pole gate. This reserve is pleasant to walk in, being mostly beech with very little undergrowth, but unfortunately it leads nowhere, so the path you take is into the untidier, denser wood; the unmarked footpath to the left of of the bridle path.

You will be walking in this wood for about a quarter of a mile, until it thins out and you find yourself with springy turf underfoot. Now you have the best part before you, a downhill walk back around the side of Wainhill to the house with the white gates that lies athwart the Icknield Way, with magnificent views to the end. The path is narrow, no more than a track, and winds about going from woods to green turf. Keep well to your left, ignoring any paths that intrude from the right. You cannot go too far left at this end of the walk as you are prevented by a fence, just as later you will be prevented by steep, rough ground. Here are the views you have been waiting for; glorious views over Chinnor, far below, and Thame, and the Vale of Aylesbury. There are places to picnic up here on Wainhill and pleasant hours can be spent exploring, but mark your path home first.

After a while the fence on the left finishes, the ground starts to fall away and becomes rough and broken. You will still be walking on turf, until the path divides before you. The footpath stays up on the ridge and the bridle path goes down into a hollow some 10 feet below. These paths run together but the ridge path is more exciting, and if you stay on it you will keep the lovely views a little longer. However, it is on bare chalk, narrow and slippery with a steep slope on either side. If you are with children you may feel it wiser to sacrifice the view for the sake of safety and take the lower path. Back again at the house with white gates, you can now either go back through the gate and across the fields to the pub, or extend the walk to 6½ miles.

6½ mile walk

To complete the walk in style, go along the Icknield Way as described in the 2½ mile walk. This will add just over a mile to the walk, but it is well worth it. In either walk you will have had a walk to remember, and that view from Wainhill will be with you for many a day. This is a marvellous walk to take in the late autumn to finish off the walking season. The trees are in glorious colour with rustly leaves underfoot, and the memory of the view can be recalled all winter long till spring comes round again.

Area 8

Whiteleaf Cross, Pulpit Hill, Great
and Little Kimble, Longdown,
Whiteleaf Hill—2 or 5 miles

AREA 8

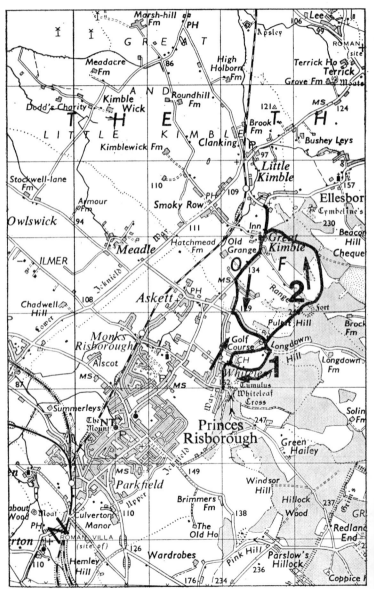

Crown copyright

Scale 1:50,000

Whiteleaf Cross, Pulpit Hill, Great and Little Kimble, Longdown, Whiteleaf Hill
2 or 5 miles

How to get there: By road from Monks Risborough.

Refreshments: "The Plough" inn, or "The Barnard Arms" hotel.

What to see: Whiteleaf Cross; the Fort of Cunobelinus; the two churches at Great and Little Kimble.

ALONG the road that runs through the woods from Monks Risborough to Princes Risborough, crossing the A4010, is the Buckinghamshire County Council's car park at Whiteleaf. Once on the right road the car park is easy to find, but choosing the right road from the mass of minor roads criss-crossing this part of rural Buckinghamshire can be difficult. The road you want passes Monks Risborough Station Halt on the left and goes towards Whiteleaf Cross, although you do not, in fact, take the turn-off to Whiteleaf village. You carry on past this turning, and the car park is half a mile further on, on the left. (Grid reference No. G.R. 820040 Ordnance Survey map, 1:50,000 series.) It is worth taking the trouble to find this starting point as this is one of the best walks in the area.

From the car park you can enjoy a pleasant stroll over Whiteleaf Hill to the Plough Inn at Longdown and back up through the woods again, or take a longer walk over the hills to Kimble to see the magnificent 13th century wall paintings at the Church of All Saints, or the burial place of John Hampden at the Church of St. Nicholas.

2 mile walk
Strike out from the car park into the picnic area, and as

you pass the last of the attractive oak benches and tables you will see a fence over to the right. Carry on through the wood, keeping this fence more or less in view, until you come out on to the greensward on the top of Whiteleaf Hill. Cut deep into the chalk below the rise is Whiteleaf Cross. The Cross itself is best viewed from below, but if you stand by its chalky hollows on a brisk spring day with the ground falling steeply away before your feet and the wind zipping around you, and look out across the peaceful vale, you will think there is no better view or more exhilarating spot in all England.

You have been following the Ridgeway Path up through the woods; here it bends away to the right through a gate in the fence. Let it go as you will find it again on the way back. The path you are taking lies ahead, a broad, grassy way across the hill, leaving the Cross behind you.

Ignoring all ways off, keep to this path as it runs downhill into a copse, rises over a small mound, then goes steeply down towards a picket fence at the bottom. Turn right at this fence, then left past the golf clubhouse and on a little distance down the gravel path to the cricket pavilion. Turn sharp right across the front of the pavilion and make for the kissing gate leading on to the golf course. There is a footpath straight across the golf course to the high green wire fence opposite where a stile leads on to a narrow path alongside a pretty thatched cottage. This wooded path runs now uphill and then down, over another stile, and brings you out eventually at the Plough inn on the Cadsden Road, where, should it be open, refreshments may be obtained. If you are taking the shorter walk, rejoin the directions given for the 5 mile walk at the point where they return to the Plough.

5 mile walk

At the Plough inn turn left along the road for some 200 yards until, on your right, you find a small post box on a telegraph pole. Just past this there is a Ridgeway sign pointing you up a steep, narrow path which runs between wire fences cutting you off from the wooded gardens of one bungalow immediately to your left and another some way up on a rise to your right. This path is not very obvious and needs searching for; if you have walked more than 400 yards along the road from the Plough you will have passed it and must turn back.

At the top of this steep little path you come on to rough meadowland. Either turn right on to the path which skirts the meadow, or strike out across it towards the far right-hand corner, where a Ridgeway plinth marks the exit. Crossing this field in spring or early summer you will be able to find millions of tiny wild pansies or heartsease. The whole field is carpeted with them.

On leaving this meadow, turn right on to the obvious path, then left within 50 yards where another path crosses. Over the style ahead, and right again on to Pulpit Hill. Follow the fence on your right, and as this fence ends you will see some way off on your right, the earthworks of an ancient Fort. This Fort, so Vera Burden tells us in "Chiltern Villages", was built by Cunobelinus, King of the Britons in the first century. Further off on the hills above Kimble is Cymbeline's Mount, and down below in the valley Cymbeline's Cottage which you will pass later.

Having investigated the Fort, rejoin your path, up a little rise, then over a stile and straight on up again for a few more yards. Here you leave the Ridgeway and turn left on to a well-beaten path which runs downhill for half a mile or so to the A4010 at Great Kimble. Turn right on to the road, and opposite you will see the ancient, ivy-covered Church of St. Nicholas. Restored in Victorian times, this little church is not as outstanding as its sister church along the road, but it is renowned as the spot where "Ship Money" Hampden formally refused to pay, thus questioning the King's right to levy unjust taxes and precipitating the Civil War. His original Document of Protest hangs, framed, in the Church of St. Nicholas to this day, giving a little thrill to any student of history.

Across the road from the church is the Barnard Arms hotel, where refreshments may be obtained, and some 200 yards further along the A4010 is the Kimble War Memorial and the Church of All Saints, Little Kimble. This beautifully kept 13th century church is blessed with magnificent medieval wall paintings and floor tiles, well worth walking to see.

On leaving this church, retrace your steps back along the road towards Great Kimble, and passing the footpath that brought you down from Pulpit Hill, proceed along the verge of the A4010 for half a mile until you come to a broad entrance on the left with two footpath signs. Take the lower of the two footpaths, passing a thatched cottage on your left. This path brings you out to the Cadsden Road at Whiteleaf village, where you turn left to walk back to the Plough inn. *(This is the point at which those taking the shorter route rejoin the walk.)*

To complete the 2 mile walk

Crossing in front of the Plough, the route turns right into the woods, up a path between the inn and adjoining car park. A Ridgeway sign points the way, and all the way over the hill and back to the Whiteleaf car park you will find little white Ridgeway Acorns painted here and there on the trees. As you enter the wood by the Plough the path forks. You take the left fork here, and the right fork when the path again divides. There is a fairly steep but very pleasant climb before you get through this quiet beechwood.

At the top of the hill the path goes through a gate on to Whiteleaf Hill, where you once again cross the green and enter the woods on your left to retrace your steps back to the picnic area.

Area 9

Wendover, Coombe Hill, Dunsmore,
Wendover—6 miles
Wendover, Coombe Hill, Lodge Hill,
Wendover—4 miles

AREA 9

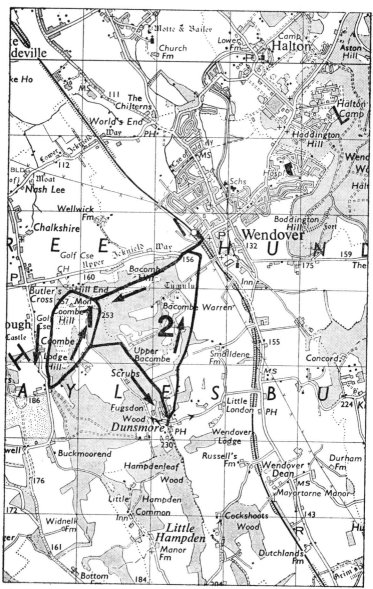

Crown copyright

Scale 1:50,000

Area 9

**Wendover, Coombe Hill, Dunsmore, Wendover
6 miles
and
Wendover, Coombe Hill, Lodge Hill, Wendover
4 miles**

How to get there: By train to Wendover Station (Baker Street to Aylesbury), or by car. Ample parking space at the Station car park.

Refreshments: Friar Tuck restaurant or several inns in Wendover; The Fox, or The Black Horse in Dunsmore.

THIS walk takes us up to the highest point in the Chilterns, the Boer War Monument on Coombe Hill, then either through the woods overlooking Butlers Cross and back round the National Trust land on Lodge Hill, or on to Dunsmore for a glimpse of the ducks on the pond and refreshments at the Fox or the Black Horse before returning to Wendover.

Both walks

Leaving Wendover Station and car park by the Shoulder of Mutton, turn right over the railway bridge into Ellesborough Road. After 300 yards or so you come to an obvious group of paths on the left marked by footpath and Ridgeway Path signs. Take the right hand path (but not the one that runs along the back of the houses in Ellesborough Road). A short, sharp climb brings you out on to Bacombe Hill. Continue to climb, and as you get towards the top of the hill the country becomes more open and the path vanishes, but keep on over the springy turf in the same direction until you come to a wooden barrier crossing the hill. Under or over this barrier (noting the acorn waymark on a tall post) brings you into the copse. Go over the stile at the top and you catch your first glimpse of the Monument ahead.

Proceed along this path, over another stile guarded by a muddy ditch, and you come out again into open country and Coombe Hill proper. The Boer War Monument is clear ahead of you, marking at 832 ft. the highest point in the Chiltern Hills.

It is obvious why Coombe Hill is so popular; a wide stretch of high heath with marvellous views across the vale, it is a superb place for a picnic, for running around with a ball, or on all but the stillest days, for flying a kite.

As you come up to the Monument you will notice a small stone plinth to the right of the path marked "Ridgeway". These plinths mark the path from here all the way over the hill. Follow them, leaving the Monument behind on your left, until you see ahead of you a wire fence crossing the hill. Here the path is not too clear, but if you bear away to the right as the fence comes into view, downhill towards a small copse in the left-hand corner, you will find the path running steeply down through the copse in the direction of Butlers Cross. Follow it if you are taking the shorter walk, but if you are intent on the long walk through Dunsmore then ignore the next few directions until the end of the 4 mile walk.

4 mile walk

Having arrived at the foot of the hill you keep to the Ridgeway, still indicated by acorn waymarks, turning sharp left through a gate into the wood. The path winds through this wood for about half a mile, when it comes out on to a road. Turn left again on to the road for a few yards, and left once again at the road sign "Dunsmore $1\frac{1}{2}$ m.". Walk along this lane at the edge of the woods for about half a mile and you will come to a parking area where three lanes join. This is the motorist's lay-by for Coombe Hill; on most fine weekends and during school holidays it is likely that you will find an ice-cream van there.

The short walk now takes you through the five-barred gate on your left on to the National Trust land at Lodge

Hill. Any of the paths facing you will lead you back towards the Monument, and thence over Coombe Hill to Wendover. *(End of 4 mile walk.)*

6 mile walk

Those who are going on to Dunsmore should leave the Ridgeway Path at Grid Reference 853068 before it goes down through the copse towards Butlers Cross, and at the fence turn left, keeping the fence parallel on your right, until you come to the five-barred gate and National Trust sign on Lodge Hill. Here you go through the gate and ignoring both the road (which goes to Dunsmore) and the broad path to your left, you take the signposted footpath through the wood opposite. At first this path runs parallel with the road to Dunsmore, but after a hundred yards or so it begins to bear left. It winds and twists about through the wood for some quarter of a mile, and though narrow it is plain to follow. Eventually it takes you over a bank and on to a bridle path. Turn right here, and follow the path and the wire fence that borders it on the left, for the mile or so through the wood into Dunsmore.

As you walk towards Dunsmore you come upon a sudden proliferation of wire fences which seem to spring up all around you. Take note of these fences as later on they mark the beginning of the way back.

The next landmark is a white house ahead of you. Take the paved path to the right of this house, and ignoring the footpath sign, carry on down the path for a few yards to the Fox inn on your right, where you can get refreshments. Alternatively, the Black Horse, 100 yards on and over the crossroads also serves refreshments. In either event, it is worth the short walk to the crossroads for a sight of the ducks and geese on Dunsmore village pond.

To return to Wendover, you go back past the Fox and the white house to the group of fences mentioned earlier. Here the path you followed from Lodge Hill is straight ahead of you going north. Almost alongside and bearing north-east is a broad track across fields, marked off by posts. This track must be a good 12 ft. wide; follow it across the fields and into a wood, where it narrows and turns right, runs downhill for some 50 yards and brings you to a beech wood on your left. Continue in a north-easterly direction through this beech wood for about a mile, ignoring the new stile on your right as you go, until you come to the end of the wood and cross a stile into rolling meadowland. Here you take the obvious path leading diagonally across the meadow to another stile. Over this stile, but do not take the path ahead of you this time, but go diagonally left again, up a short, steep rise to yet another stile and a path taking you straight across the middle of a ploughed field towards a row of houses in the distance. Between these houses, go through a gate and on to the road. Turn right for 50 yards until you find a footpath sign on the left. Go through the gate or over the stile here, and follow the footpath between the pylons until it brings you back on to the Ellesborough Road, opposite the Shoulder of Mutton and Wendover Station, to complete a walk of just over 6 miles.

Area 10

Tring, Ivinghoe, Tring—5$\frac{1}{2}$, 9$\frac{1}{2}$ or 4$\frac{1}{2}$ miles

AREA 10

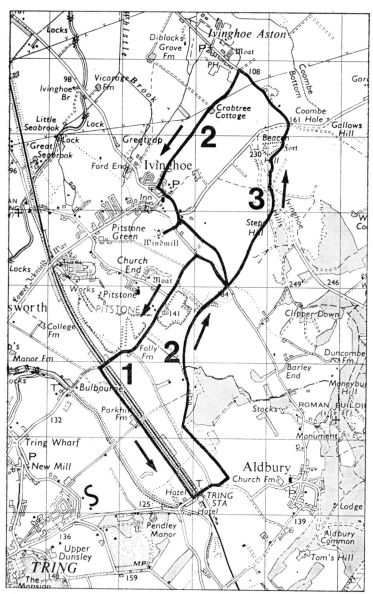

Crown copyright

Scale 1:50,000

Area 10

Tring, Ivinghoe, Tring
5½, 9½ or 4½ miles

How to get there: For 5½ and 9½ mile walks, by train to Tring Station, Euston to Bletchley line. For 4½ miles walk, by car to car park at Grid Reference 954150 on Ridgeway Path south of Ivinghoe on the road to Aldbury.

Refreshments: Silver Birch cafe; Rose & Crown in Ivinghoe; Royal Hotel at Tring Station.

FROM Ivinghoe to Tring is the stretch where the Chiltern Ridgeway most resembles its Berkshire counterpart. Here again is the chalky path striding across downland, but kindlier to the foot and eye; the bare ribs of chalk are covered with springy turf and the hills are softly wooded, greener and more rounded. It is glorious walking country, the way is scattered with wild flowers from February to October, and in spring and early summer the woods and hedges are fluffy with roses.

Two of the walks in this area start from Tring Station (on the Euston to Bletchley line), where there is also a large car park for those who come by road. The third walk starts from the car park at Grid Reference 954150.

5½ and 9½ mile walks

On leaving Tring Station, turn right over the bridge, pass the car park and continue along the road, bearing right slightly where the Pitstone road joins. You will see a large bungalow situated in the fields up on your left; take the bridleway up towards this bungalow, keeping straight on by the hedge when the paved road turns left. Ahead the Ridgeway Path crosses, and on reaching it you turn left.

This section of the Ridgeway has been hewn through the middle of a thick hedge. After a while the path opens out giving a view across fields on the left to the railway beyond. Shortly the path turns right at a chestnut tree and begins to wind uphill. As you come into a copse, look out for the Ridgeway signpost directing you up a narrow path across a steep bank on your left, into a dip and up on to a path which crosses a rough, steep field towards a footpath sign ahead. Passing the footpath sign you again enter the wood and pass on in both sun and shadow through a cloud of roses in summertime, going gradually upwards.

As you leave the wood, a footpath sign directs you ahead around the shoulder of the hill. Down in the valley are peaceful farms with Pitstone Cement Works looming ahead; the path is bordered with rabbit holes, and in early summer the whole heath is yellow with cowslips scattered in the grass. After crossing the next stile you ignore the obvious path ahead and make your way diagonally right across the hill towards the ridge. Here the way follows the wire fence along the crown of the hill until the fence runs away into scrub, when you cross the rise before you either by the path that goes over or the path that goes round. Both lead to a stile ahead, giving on to a road.

Those on the longer walk will cross the road to the downs on the other side and continue ahead.

5½ mile walk

For this walk turn left on to the road where a downhill walk of half a mile will bring you to the Silver Birch cafe. Turn left again as you come to the Tring road crossing, and the cafe is 50 yards along on the right. Leaving the cafe, turn right on to the rather busy Tring road for another 50 yards or so, when you will find yourself safe on the broad verge. The route runs for 1 mile along this verge, until, just past a turning off on the left to Aldbury, the road narrows to cross a railway bridge. Immediately over this bridge a footpath on the left runs beside the railway back to Tring Station. *(End of the 5½ mile walk.)*

To complete 9½ mile walk and commence 4½ mile walk

Having crossed the road at Grid Reference 954150 those on the longer walk will follow the Ridgeway Path signs over stiles and across pasture, keeping company with the sheep, until the path broadens between hawthorn bushes, becoming bare and chalky underfoot and begins to climb the hill in earnest. Climb over the gate at the top and continue on along the now easier path, separated by a fence on the left from the National Trust Ashridge Estate. Soon you will see ahead of you the summit of Ivinghoe Beacon.

Coming to a road, you cross over and walk through the car park to where Ridgeway acorn marks show you the way through a post and chain fence and on to the chalky path that climbs the Beacon. Here on the top of the hill, with marvellous views in all directions, the Ridgeway Long Distance Footpath finishes, the end as unmarked as was the start at Overton Hill. Should you decide to picnic up here enjoying the views, and then return along the Ridgeway to Tring Station as you came, you will have walked 8 miles over some of the best walking country in the Chiltern Hills, but for this third round walk you skirt round to the right of the hill where the path leads you on with your face towards the lion carved into the chalk of the hill opposite. After 100 yards you will come to a gate; do not pass through it but take the path going steeply downhill left which descends to the Dunstable road at a junction. Take the minor road opposite signposted "Ivinghoe Aston", and walk along the road for the best part of 1 mile until you come to the outskirts of the village. Here you turn left into the lane that leads you past Crabtree Cottage, and thence to Ivinghoe. The hedgerows here are a mass of elderflower and dog roses in summer, and rabbits bound across the path.

Arriving at Ivinghoe village, continue along the road ahead to the Rose and Crown, which lies at the junction of Wellcroft and Vicarage Lane. After refreshment you turn left into Vicarage Lane to the junction with High Street, where the way again goes left. Proceed along the road, ignoring the Dunstable Road coming in from the left, to a footpath sign and a low stile on your left.

At this point you should make a diversion to visit the Pitstone windmill, now restored to working order by the Chiltern Society, and well worth inspection.

The walk continues on the footpath leading between fences for 200 yards or so, over another low stile, alongside a hedge skirting a cornfield, and over yet another stile on to the downs again. If you look over to your right as you cross this stile you will see the scar of a chalk pit in the distance. Make diagonally across the downs towards it, and you will find yourself back at the two stiles and the road where the short walk turned left. You have rejoined the Ridgeway path, which you can follow back to Tring Station.

Note: 4½ mile walk

For this walk you should park in the car park at Grid Reference 954150, where the Ridgeway Path crosses the road between Ivinghoe and Aldbury. From this point follow the route given for the 9½ mile walk, for a round walk over the Beacon and through Ivinghoe, back to the car park.

BIBLIOGRAPHY

SPURBOOKS publish a series of books on various long distance footpaths and local walks and rambles.

The following books provide further reading on the Ridgeway Footpath:

The Prehistoric Ridgeway—Patrick Crampton—Abbey Press.

Chiltern Villages—V. B. Burden—Spurbooks.

Companion into Berkshire—R. P. Beckinsale—Spurbooks.

A Guide to the Prehistoric and Roman Monuments in England and Wales—Jacquetta Hawkes—Cardinal Paperbacks.

The Thames Valley—Frank Martin—Spurbooks.

Country Like This—Friends of the Vale of Aylesbury—F. Weatherhead & Son.

ALSO IN THIS SERIES
OF
FOOTPATH GUIDES

Available from all good local Bookshops